MW01167604

Hope Beyond Bars

An Inmate's Journey to True Freedom

JEDIDIAH DUAYA

authorHOUSE®

AuthorHouse™
1663 Liberty Drive
Bloomington, IN 47403
www.authorhouse.com
Phone: 1 (800) 839-8640

THE HOLY BIBLE, NEW INTERNATIONAL VERSION®, NIV® Copyright © 1973, 1978, 1984, 2011 by Biblica, Inc.® Used by permission. All rights reserved worldwide.

Published by AuthorHouse 06/20/2018

ISBN: 978-1-5462-4751-7 (sc)
ISBN: 978-1-5462-4750-0 (e)

Foreword

One of the most difficult experiences I consistently face as a full-time jail chaplain is the inability to assist inmates in reentering society. One lady was being released at the coldest time of the year. She was arrested in summer and thus had no appropriate attire for the bone-chilling temperatures she was about to face. Her boyfriend had found another love and had rid himself of almost all the inmate's possessions. Her mother passed two weeks before her release, and with her mother's passing went the only residence she had available. No finances, no roof over her head, no transportation, no food, and no friends to pick her up when she was to be dropped off at the courthouse.

My heart was touched. I solicited the assistance of some others, and almost all the needs were to be met. On the day of her release, the sun began its descent, and the temperature began to plummet. On the coldest night of the year, her anticipated time of release came and went. Seems an "issue" was raised that needed resolved before she could be let go.

The "issue" was finally resolved, and she was taken to the city of her arrest and put on the street. The hands on the town clock displayed the dismal situation. Too late. The church with the coat and food had closed. Where would she get something to keep her from freezing? How was she to get around town? What was she to eat? Where could she get money to buy food? Where could she go to escape the blistering cold?

With my twelve years of experience as jail chaplain and a total of over twenty-three years in jail ministry, I have seen this scenario play out countless times. Reentry is a gorilla that is almost impossible to get one's arms around—housing, transportation, food, clothing, employment, medicine, how to obtain adequate attire for job interviews, and the list goes on.

I have seen success on rare occasions. Yes, some companies are willing to hire ex-offenders. Yes, there are churches willing to help. Yes, there are some programs available. Yes, there are shelters and halfway houses. But far from enough. Jedidiah Duaya's desire is to encourage and inspire those outside the walls of jails and prisons to step up to the plate and help in whatever way they can.

The phone rang in my office in February 2016, and I first heard the voice of Jedidiah Duaya, a man I would come to respect and value as a friend. In his first email to me, he expressed a concern for inmates while in the jail and subsequent to release. During our first conversation, it was obvious that Jedidiah was honestly concerned for the welfare of inmates. He came to the jail; we walked the halls, talked about inmates, discussed the chaplain's ministry, and considered programs available to inmates. Since this meeting, Jedidiah continues to take the stand that something needs to be done for the inmates, particularly in the area of reentry.

Myself and another staff member from the jail appeared on Jedidiah's radio program to voice to the general public some of the obstacles and opportunities available. Our prayer was that God would speak to hearts and motivate individuals, churches, and businesses to get involved.

This work by Jedidiah Duaya is a continuation of the desire of his heart and the determination in his soul to arouse society in general and the church specifically to awake, arise, and assist inmates. We recently had lunch, and I heard much the same as I did two years ago—in essence, "Chaplain, I want to see society and the church get involved." Jedidiah is aware of the revolving-door culture of inmates and is intent on using all his talents as a talk show host and author to help "the least of these." It is easy to talk the talk, but Jedidiah walks the walk, as evidenced by the content of this book.

He takes us from birth to decisions to consequences to incarceration to a new birth. Along the way, he encourages society and the church to get involved and make a difference in a soul. I encourage each one who reads this book to follow his advice.

It may be that the next inmate released on a very cold night will be released in your town, reside in your neighborhood, visit your church, and need your assistance. With Jedidiah's advice, one can start preparing to be used of the Lord to ensure the events of our lady inmate will not repeat themselves.

Chaplain Gene C. Sayre Jr.
Hampton Roads Regional Jail
AS, BRE, MRE

Hope beyond Bars

An Inmate's Journey to True Freedom

In this life, none of us comes here with less than the next person in line. We are all born of God. We all have the same Creator. We all have the same God at the time of our birth. We all are under the care of one parent or both parents, of one grandparent or both grandparents, of a foster parent, and the list goes on. But we do not grow or shape ourselves with no outside influence whatsoever. Nobody grows old independent of outside influences.

Now, I want to clarify here that these influences can be good or bad, and these influences will be reflected in our behaviors and actions in our childhood and into adult life. While it is true that we all have the same birth experience with the same Creator, the truth is that once we make it through the birth canal, not all of us will have the same upbringing. Some will have golden spoons. Some will have silver spoons. Some will have nothing. From the moment we arrive here, our lives will no longer be the same as our next-door neighbors'. Behind the four walls of our homes hide a lot of secrets that the outside world cannot comprehend.

Some of us will have a choice about what to eat, while others will have no choice at all. Some of us will wear designer clothes imported from overseas, while others will wear secondhand clothing. Some of us will sleep in an expensive crib, while others will reuse their sibling's crib or even a gifted crib, and maybe some of us will have no place to sleep and will end up sleeping with our parents on their bed.

Once we have grown out of being toddlers, we are faced with education. Some of us will go to pre-K, others will go to an expensive day care, and still others will stay at home with a parent—not by choice but because of limited finances. Some of us will have new attire to wear each school year, while for others, the new school year means a time of depression because it reminds them of their lack of money. And then once we become aware of Thanksgiving, and especially of Christmas, where exchanging gifts is the norm for some, we experience a time of discouragement and even depression. While some of us have a list of gifts we want, others have no idea what they want and are satisfied with whatever is presented to them—and maybe they'll receive nothing at all.

And then we become teenagers and have a whole new set of desires and wants. Some's desires and wants are met without them even expressing them, while for others, these desires and wants don't even cross their minds, because they have never had anything of the sort. Then we hear our classmates talk about their gifts, while others sit there quiet and in shame for not receiving anything. Notice that all of this adds up and shapes us. Some will take this life experience easily as it comes and cherish every moment, while others will take this in disdain, reject it, and turn bitter toward life itself.

Now, we have just passed the preteenage years, and we are entering into young adulthood, or adolescence (I am talking fifteen years old and up for the most part). We have all these aforementioned issues in our hearts and minds, and we have been dealing with these for a while now. But we have hope at the end. We have no example to follow, and we have no one to look up to. We live life by going whichever way the wind blows. We have kept all this stuff in us. We might have a fear of sharing it with others, since they might not be trustworthy afterward or they might use this information against us. Or we may not know how to share our feelings, so we end up keeping all of this inside us.

After a while, we have to find an escape. Sex becomes our escape. Taking what doesn't belong to us becomes our escape. Terrorizing people becomes our escape. Bullying and harassing people becomes our escape. The negatives of our upbringing have been simmering in us for so long, and they have gotten to a boiling point, and they have to escape; we have to let out that negativity, but we are not trained to do that in a positive way, so we let it out in the only way we know.

Rape is not excluded here. Murder is not excluded here. Bank robbery is not excluded here. Breaking and entering is not excluded here. So we do it the first time, and we do not get caught. We do it the second time, and we still do not get caught. We are now excited, and we do it the third time—and we do not get caught. And now, it has become part of our lives. Now, we are untouchable.

And the more we are involved in these activities, the more they become part of us. And not only that, these criminal behaviors become us; these behaviors become our identities, and the earlier someone gets involved in these lifestyles, the deeper these bad behaviors can take root as time goes on.

The environment in which someone grows up will always play a big part in the individual's life. For example, an abused person often will end up abusing others. An individual who has been cheated on will often end up cheating. You can grow and live your life in a circle; it will end up influencing part of your life, and you will eventually act accordingly.

None of us will live life on this side of heaven without making mistakes. Mistakes are part of life. We cannot experience life without stumbling and fumbling. We are not perfect, nor are we expected to be perfect, and we should not feel bad about that. Christ dealt with this issue when asked about who is good, and Christ answered that no one is good except the Father. And Christ stated that we should be as perfect as our Father in heaven is perfect.

Be as Perfect as Your Father in Heaven

While we are not expected to be good, at the same time, we are expected to be as perfect as our Father in heaven is. This is not contradictory but instead paradoxical. In other words, what Christ tells us is that we are to be perfect in *Him* only.

This perfection is impossible apart from Christ; it is possible in Christ alone. Only in Christ can we be perfect and be like our Father in heaven.

The truth of the matter is that apart from Christ, we cannot be or do anything that is asked or expected of us in God. We cannot live a righteous life apart from God. We cannot live a Christian life apart from the Creator or apart from Christ Himself. We cannot refrain from committing crimes apart from Christ. We cannot refrain from cheating on our spouses or cheating on our taxes apart from our Creator. You may be good in your own eyes, but are you good in the eyes of your Creator? It is impossible to be perfect apart from God, your Creator.

When it is asked of us to forgive our enemies, this is humanly impossible, except with Christ, with whom it is possible. Christ told us to give and it shall be given unto us as a principle to prosperity, and it is impossible for a person to do this without Christ's help.

Let me emphasize here that we are to do and achieve everything in Christ alone, and this also includes being perfect, being holy, and living a Christian life. Everything God asks us to be and do is possible and achievable only in Christ.

We are destined to succeed, and we are destined to stumble and make mistakes as well. But what we are not destined to do or expected to do is quit. God created us in His own image and likeness, and God expects us to live life accordingly. God not only expects us to live life in His own image and likeness on earth, God also expects us to make mistakes, even though we are in His image and likeness. But we are never to be God, and while making those mistakes, we are not to dwell on them. People can make mistakes, but they have to dust themselves off and get up and get moving. A mistake is not the end, but neither should it be an invitation to continue on with a life of sins.

Since we are not God ourselves, and because we are human beings, God expects us to stumble sometimes. God knows we will make mistakes sometimes, but what God doesn't expect from us is for us to quit. Quitting should never be mentioned in any area of our lives. No matter what happens in our lives, and no matter what we might face, we should never quit.

No Matter What, Never Quit on Yourself

No matter what crime you might have committed, no matter what mistakes you might have made, and no matter what you might have done to yourself or to your neighbor, one thing you should never do is quit on yourself. The key to a successful life is to never quit on life, never quit on yourself, and never quit on your neighbor.

You have to fight for yourself. You have to fight for what you believe. You have to fight for your neighbor. Quitting should not be an option. Always fight, fight, and fight some more. Never quit, never quit, never quit! Even as you sit in a jail or prison cell, serving time, no matter how long that time is, you should not quit on yourself just because you are inside those four walls.

Society might quit on you, your friends and family might quit on you, but as long as you don't quit on yourself, you'll be just fine. This is also verified and confirmed in Christ, when He went through His tough time at Golgotha where His friends, His disciples, all quit on Him. Some betrayed Him, some rejected Him, and some doubted Him, but as long as Christ never quit on Himself, He was able to overcome all the behavior of His circle.

This is the same behavior I want all readers, and especially my fellow inmates, to walk away with: never quit on yourself, because once you quit on yourself, who else will be there for you? If and when you quit on yourself, everything that your Creator prepared and planned for you to fulfill on earth will not be achieved nor fulfilled.

David messed up, but he never quit on himself. Adam messed up but never quit on himself. Moses messed up as well but never quit on himself. Abram messed up but never quit on himself. Peter messed up but never quit on himself. You have messed up, you have committed crimes, and you have done wrong, but you should not quit on yourself. Quitting on yourself is the last thing you should consider in your life. Besides avoiding temptation to quit on yourself, you also need to avoid, or at least try to avoid, quitting on your God.

Don't Give Up on God, Because He Won't Give Up on You

While I was penning this book, especially this portion, the words of this song, "He's Able," came to mind, as it was a confirmation of this portion of the book. No matter what you have done and no matter how society has judged you for your deeds, do not give up on yourself, and most importantly, do not give up on God. Many people will have a hard time admitting they have given up on God, but maybe—just maybe—if you give me some of your precious time and reason with me in the next few lines, you will come to this conclusion.

Have you ever blamed God for what has happened to you or your family? Have you ever turned resentful and bitter toward God for what you are enduring or for the price you are paying because of your past mistakes? If you answer yes to these questions, then yes, you have indeed begun to quit on God. It is easy to quit on yourself. And it is easier to quit on your God, because now, you have the chance to accuse someone who cannot defend Himself in your regard. When you point the finger at a defenseless person, you have the temporary upper hand in your eyes, and in the eyes of your circle of friends.

Everybody blames God, because God is the easy target. Sadly, the same mindset applies to the devil; we tend to blame him as well because he cannot defend himself. It is true that God and the devil are both easy targets to blame. Since God is the only one who really cares for you and me, then we need to make up our minds that no matter what situations we find ourselves in, we need to force ourselves to focus on the goodness of God toward us. That will lead us to not quit or give up on God.

Yes, you are still locked up. Yes, your life is still controlled and guided by someone else. Yes, you still have to answer to someone for your every move, and it is not easy, but you can make this life situation smoother if you remove quitting on God from the equation.

One main reason why you should never dare quit on God is the very fact that God will never quit on you. This in itself—having a God who never quits on His creation—should send joy to our souls. If you doubt, I challenge you to name me one person in the Bible who messed up and saw God quit or give up on them. Just provide one person. I can guarantee you will not find one.

It is easy for the devil to quit on you, because he did not create you. It is easy for your family and friends to quit on you, because they did not create you. But it is very hard, even impossible, for God, your Creator, to quit on you, because not only did He create you but He also died for you to restore you unto Himself after you fell away from Him. In your dirty state, in your sentence time, in your jail cell time, you should seek to praise God for having you there. And when you decide not to quit on God, that will automatically cause you to not quit on yourself, because it is impossible to please God and please yourself.

Whether it's the crime you committed or the mistakes

you have made, or the decision to change your life, or the decision to never quit or to quit, you are the one to make the decision based on the choices presented to you. All of us have choices presented to us, and we also have the right and privilege to decide, but what we do not have is the power to define the consequences of our choices. While we might have the power to choose our decisions, we do not have the power to control the consequences of our so-called decisions.

The Power to Choose

In Deuteronomy 30:19–20, we read how God called heaven and earth to record this day against the people before whom He had set life and death, blessing and cursing. He said, "Therefore, choose life, that both thou and thy seed may live." God trusted our judgment enough to set life and death before us. This in itself is big, and it is very overwhelming. Here, you have a God who happens to be the Creator of humanity and decided not to control His own creation but gave this creation liberty to choose life or death. God did not stop there; He also gave His people a choice of whether to choose Him or to reject Him.

Now let us take a pause here and reason. You created somebody, and you decide to trust them and trust their judgment without controlling their choices or decision-making abilities. Not only is this act of God risky, but it shows how much God values us and values our thinking process. It is risky because now, the people can choose life by choosing God, or choose death by denying God. The risk is to have your creation not choose you. While it is risky on God's side, it is a show of respect for Him to trust our human judgment. Unfortunately, this freedom of judgment has led human beings to abuse their choices.

Even though God doesn't force us to choose life or choose Him, God advises us to do the right thing. By choosing Him, we therefore are choosing life. Choosing life is the right choice for all of us and all our beneficiaries as well, but guess what? Not all of humanity chooses life or chooses God.

Whether or not we like it, every action that we take will either bring us blessings or make us suffer cursings. If we lived our lives knowing that we will pay for every single deed or action, we would live our lives differently. When we use our privilege to choose as we wish, we can live accordingly, and this not only affects us but also will affect our descendants.

Let me clarify here that not choosing God is choosing death and everything that comes with it. Let me say it again: when we do not choose God, we automatically choose death. There is no middle ground or gray area. Either we choose God or we do not choose God, but we have to make a choice.

We all have the power to choose in common, and this power to choose will carry us and live out in our lives. By making choices, we will enjoy the blessings of our choices, or pay the price with a curse. Let us not just have the power to choose and not choose at all; better yet, let us make the right choice. On the contrary, let us utilize our right to choose by choosing right and following God's advice.

And God's advice is crystal clear: we should choose life and, in turn, choose Him.

When one makes a choice about a particular thing, one has to stand by that choice no matter what; otherwise, that individual will fall in the double-minded category. In life, we will always be presented with dual choices. This can be verified with Eve and Adam, when Satan tempted Eve to eat of the fruits of the garden. Eve faced a choice between eating the fruit and not eating it, between good and evil.

David also faced such a choice when dealing with Beersheba. Instead of going to war and leading his people to victory, Mr. King David chose to remain in the house. Bored, he decided to take a walk, when he suddenly saw a beautiful woman who caught his attention and led him to have an affair with her. David was presented with a choice between pursuing the woman and staying away from her, and he chose to go after her and commit adultery.

We can also find an example in Judas, when he received money to betray Christ with a kiss. Judas looked for an occasion to accomplish that. Once the opportunity presented itself, Judas had a choice to either actualize his desire or ignore it and move on. As we all know, Judas followed through with his thoughts and chose to commit betrayal.

We can conclude that all the people in these few examples

were faced with choices, and they all decided to act on their choices.

Our Choices and Decisions

A distinction should be made here between choices and decisions. We make our choices first; then, we take our decisions. Choices always precede decisions. When presented with a challenge, we choose to act a certain way, but our actions ought to be followed by a decision on our part.

Let me clarify: we can choose to go to a particular restaurant and receive a menu and choose our meal. We have not chosen what to eat just yet, but we have decided to eat and live with the consequences.

The point I am trying to make is that everything we do ought to be preceded with a choice and followed by a decision. We choose, and then we decide to act on our choices. This process is very critical in anyone's life. If we can win the battles of our choices, we can carry those wins in our decisions. Our decisions will always be the results of our choices.

Let me bring some clarity one more time. You are shopping for a vehicle, and you go to a dealership. Once you arrive, you have a choice of thousands of vehicles in the lot. Now you have to choose, but you still have not decided yet. Once you have chosen a make or a model of a brand and the year and the mileage, then and only then can you move forward and decide to purchase a vehicle.

You might have a date with a lady friend, and a perverted thought crosses your mind. Now, you have a choice to pursue those thoughts or not. But in your pursuit, you still have not decided to act on those thoughts yet. Only when you decide on your choice can you decide to act. As a reminder here, those decisions will bear consequences.

The Consequences of Our Choices

As stated earlier, each of our actions will bear consequences, good or bad. It is amazing how we celebrate the freedom that we have and our power to choose but we become disgruntled and unhappy when we are told that we will reap the harvest of our choices. If we want the freedom to choose, we should also be ready to bear the consequences of the choices made.

I can confirm that all the people of God described above had one thing in common, besides their being presented with choices; after making their choices and deciding to follow through with them, they all paid the price for their choices.

- Eve chose and decided to eat of the fruits of the knowledge of good and evil, and she paid the price by being separated from God the Father. And the consequences were not to be lived by her nor Adam alone, but by her descendants, which include you and me.
- David chose and decided to avoid going to war and instead remain in his house, specifically on top of the roof, and he went after the woman in temptation and fell in sin. David could have chosen not to

fall for that, but he decided otherwise, and when confronted by God through the prophet Nathan, David paid the price, stripped of his kingdom. And his descendants also paid a heavy price, where death became the norm, where incest and adultery became the norm, and where the sword was now part of his kingdoms and family.

- Judas chose to take the offer to betray his Lord and actually decided to sell out his Lord. Judas could have opted to remain faithful to his Lord but went the other way and accepted thirty pieces of silver. When he realized his actions were not what he wanted, he decided to return the money, but it was too late; it had already cost him his life.

- Peter was presented with the opportunity to deny his Lord, and he chose and decided to deny him not only one time but three times at that, and this cost him his life, even though Peter's actions were a fulfillment of old-time prophecies.

If all our bad actions can cause us to pay a price in our lives and in our descendants' lives, guess what? All our good actions will cause us to enjoy life, and our descendants will have a future with guaranteed success. To gain deeper insight on this subject, I encourage you to read my book titled *Dying in Good Old Age*, where I deal with this topic in depth.

While we have the power to choose, and we will definitely live with either the consequences or the blessings of our choices and decisions, we need to be aware that when we find ourselves on the other side of our choices and decisions, we have to focus our attention there. Making a mistake or mistakes is not the end of the world. If we stumble and fall short of the will of God, it is not the end of the world. The end of the world is when we decide to remain in the same place after our bad decisions.

The Mistake of Life

The mistake of life is not making the mistake itself, or the mistakes themselves. The mistake of life is not getting back on track after falling sideways in the journey of God in this life. Whatever your mistake is—whatever you have done that you now know to have been a mistake—do not remain in it or dwell on it.

You have messed up. You have fallen short. You committed adultery. You committed murder. You might have raped someone. You have stolen and gotten caught. You were busted in a drug deal. You cheated on your spouse and got caught. I mean, whatever it is that you have done, I want you to know and understand that even though you made those mistakes, you are not a mistake. And since you are not a mistake, you have hope, and you can live again, way past your actual mistakes.

Yes, you have done all those things, and you have made all those mistakes. Yes, you have committed all those crimes, but to dwell on them is the mistake of life that could hurt you even worse and keep you stuck in life, as opposed to moving forward.

I wrote this book with the goal to reach inmates and help society deal with inmates. Most importantly, I wrote this book for anyone who has made some mistakes, and I encourage those people not to remain in them. I need the inmates who have this book handy to understand that they had a choice in a certain time of their lives, and they decided to act a certain way, which turned out to be a mistake. And they just happened to get caught and are now locked up, serving time. The mistakes were made. The crimes were committed. The sentencing was pronounced and time served. That is a fact. This should not remain as such. Life has to be lived. Life continues on even within jail walls.

I beg you, my readers, whoever you are and whatever you have done, do not dwell in your past. Even though you might have to live with the consequences of your mistakes, and those consequences might be very costly, one thing you should not do is identify yourself with the mistakes.

I Am Not "It"

One of the greatest, most effective weapons the devil has used in people's lives is his ability to cause people to identify themselves with their failures, their struggles, their sickness, their pains and hurts, and their bad experiences. You cannot move on in life with an old or wrong identity.

Here, it's important to mention how Paul the Apostle declared, "Old things are passed away; behold, all things are become new" (2 Corinthians 5:17). When Paul the Apostle says "old things," he is talking to all of us, the readers of this book. The very fact that you are reading this book tells me that you have a past, and in that past, you did some things that might have been good or bad, but the point is that you have some old things. And if those old things have to pass away, it tells me that you should not identify yourself with them. You never have to identify yourself with passing things. If they are passing, let them pass.

The next point that Paul the Apostle wants us to know is that *all* things become new. The things that you did are not only old but passed. When Paul says *all*, *all* means *all*. Whatever you did is included in *all*. Whatever you did that you are ashamed to mention to your circle of friends, even those very things are old and ought to be buried in the past. *All things* means *all things*.

All things become new. While we need to let go of the old things, we need to embrace the things that become new. We should never hold on to old, passing things, but we sure need to hold on to new, becoming things.

I want you to repeat, "I am not it, I am not it, I am not it." If you happen to have committed a murder, I want you to say to yourself, "I am not a murderer." If you happen to have committed rape, I want you to say to yourself, "I am not a rapist." If you happen to have committed an act of robbery, I want you to say, "I am not a thief." If you happen to have been caught dealing drugs, I want you to say to yourself, "I am not a drug dealer." I hope by now you have gotten my point. Whatever you do, or whatever you did, never identify yourself with it. You did it, but you are not it.

This is why a change of mind is important. We have to work hard at seeing ourselves in a different light from what we have been seen as and punished for. We always will have the power to see ourselves in any light we need to based on our Creator.

I Am Responsible

One of the first steps in any form of restoration session or counseling session is to acknowledge your mistake and take responsibility for it. Once you acknowledge your mistake and take responsibility, it marks the beginning of the journey to change. It is the start of a new life. Most people will never take responsibility for their wrongdoings and, in turn, blame everybody else. Blaming anyone but yourself will keep you from learning the lessons you need to learn in order to change for the better. While jail or prison might be your current situation, that should not be the end of the road, and the deciding factor will be your taking responsibility for your past actions. Once you do that, you will be free to forgive yourself, whether you are right or wrong. Since the system has already decided on your case, your being right or wrong has nothing to do with it. Once you take responsibility for your actions, that will be the beginning of your change.

Once you look at your life beyond the mistakes you made, and you take responsibility, you can move forward by forgiving yourself.

Forgive Yourself

We find it easier to forgive others, as we are commanded in the Bible, than to forgive ourselves. Even those who are not Bible believers practice this principle of forgiving others. Applying forgiveness to others who have harmed us or done us wrong has a true benefit. While forgiveness will set you free from others, there is also a forgiveness that will set you free from yourself and your past. Forgiving yourself will bring you to a place where you can look at yourself for who you really are through some new glasses and believe in the process of restoration, as opposed to looking at what your mistakes will try to identify you with.

There is no true restoration without self-forgiveness. You have to be able to forgive yourself and see yourself past your mistakes; only then can you receive and apply true freedom.

After forgiving yourself, you can move on to forgive those you believe might have contributed to your lockup. They might have sold you out to law enforcement. They might have snitched on you. They might have set you up to be caught. And now you are serving time. Those people deserve to be forgiven as well. As you forgive yourself, it is incumbent upon you to forgive those people too.

Remember Christ on the cross, when He faced His greatest challenges and He prayed, "Father, forgive them; for they know not what they do" (Luke 23:34). If Christ could endure all that He endured and still at the end of His journey ask the Father to forgive His betrayers, that alone should lead all of us to do likewise—and especially you, my sisters and brothers who are in jail or prison, or even under house arrest.

You should be able to apply this principle and forgive all those you believe have wronged you and even caused you to end up where you are right now. You might still be serving time, and your freedom may still not be fully restored, but you can still let them go in your heart. You don't forgive them because of them; you forgive them because your Father in heaven has forgiven you and continues to forgive you. When you forgive yourself, then you can go on and repent from them.

Repentance

We have all heard the sentence "Repentance is good for the soul." The difference here is to be made between forgiveness and repentance. While forgiveness mostly deals with your past actions or deeds that might have led you to end up where you are, repentance, on the other hand, is about your future from the moment you ask for forgiveness. We ask God to forgive us for our sins that we have committed, and then we have to repent from them; that will show in our future actions after the forgiveness step. Repentance is "Lord, I repent from lying," while forgiveness is "Lord, forgive me for lying." Forgiveness is "Father, forgive me for stealing," while repentance is "Father, I repent from stealing." Forgiveness is "Father, forgive me for cheating on my mate," while repentance is "Father, I repent from cheating."

The danger comes when one asks for forgiveness without repenting. In that case, one can still continue a sinful life even after asking for forgiveness. It is beneficial for one to start the journey by asking for forgiveness, but make sure you don't end it there; continue with the repentance step with actions to follow.

And believe it or not, a jail or prison cell or even house arrest can serve as a place to reflect on one's actions and, after asking for forgiveness, seek repentance. You can seek repentance by making up your mind that, once freed, you will not go back to old ways. Once allowed to return to society, you may say you guarantee that you will do your best, with the help of your God, not to return to old dungs. The sad truth is that most inmates will ask for forgiveness, and even repent, but will do so with the four walls in mind, meaning once they get out of their cells, they will ignore and forget all those processes they guaranteed and will eventually come back to jail, prison, or house arrest.

Lessons to Be Learned

After one repents, one has to learn the lessons from previous actions in order to keep from repeating the same mistakes that brought trouble in the first place. Lessons to be learned will always be in your mind and become the tool to keep you from acting the same way. Wherever you find yourself as a consequence of your mistakes, you have to humble yourself and stay mindful, not getting caught up in the actual situation, and learn as many lessons there are to be learned as you can.

Since you are already locked up and serving time, there is no need to feel sorry for yourself anymore, and you have no more need to find someone to blame, including you. Yes, you have taken responsibility for your actions. You have asked for forgiveness, and you have repented, but you are still locked up and still could be for more months, years, or even decades. There are some things you can do while in there.

Enjoy the Night

As the Bible declares, "Weeping may endure for a night, but joy comes in the morning" (Psalm 30:5). No matter how long the night might be, the day will eventually come. No matter how dark it is, the light will break. No matter how long you weep or cry, your tears will be wiped away.

Until your day breaks, until the light shines, until the sun rises, you are commanded by God to rejoice. David asked the question "How can I rejoice in the midst of trouble?" You might also relate to this question by asking, "How long shall my night last? How long shall my pain endure? How long shall my weeping continue?"

Jeremiah also applied this principle dealing with the Israelites. God had the Israelites exiled in a strange land. There, they served their enemies as captives as a response to their rebellious and disobedient actions. God specifically commanded the Israelites to remain in the custody of their enemies and to rejoice there. God commanded His own people to live life in a strange land. God commanded them to marry, have children, have businesses, and basically live life until He brought deliverance their way.

God asks us to rejoice while the night is still young. In the midst of your night, rejoice. The night's effect on one's life will be determined by the individual's attitude that night. How you handle the night will play a big role in your outcome that night. You can enjoy the night when you know the day will eventually break. You can enjoy the night when you know that no matter what comes your way, you can smile, because you know who holds the times and the seasons. Whether night or day, God does.

Let me share a brief story that my pastor shared. A woman who attended his church came to the pastor seeking his prayers and counsel. She had a son who was in prison for committing a crime. She sought counsel with the pastor for her son's case. While the pastor was getting ready to pray for the woman's son, the pastor was inspired by the Holy Ghost to tell the woman that her son's imprisonment was actually a blessing. And the woman was shocked to hear the pastor's statement that her son's imprisonment was a blessing. How could she rejoice with her son's imprisonment and count that as a blessing?

The question that crossed this woman's mind, and that will cross our minds as well, is "How can jail or prison be a blessing to anyone?" The pastor told the woman that her son's being in prison was a blessing because if he were outside of prison at that time, he would have died. In other words, if the son were not locked up at that time, he would already have been dead or killed due to his involvement in gang activities.

And the pastor continued on and advised the woman that she might as well rejoice that her son was locked up and alive. She would rather have him alive and locked up than free and dead. Now, I want you to hear this: "You would rather have your family member, or friend, or even yourself locked up and alive, as opposed to free and dead."

This is deep and has changed my perspective on life itself. We should see prison as a place of blessing because God, who knows everything, knew that life outside of prison would not have been worth it, not only for this woman but for all of us. Wherever we find ourselves in life, no matter what has gotten us here, we need to look at it as a place of blessing, or we need to turn it into a place of blessing. The four-wall cell that you have gotten yourself into might not look like a place of blessing, but it is, because it could be worse. Being alive is and will always be better than death.

You might have lost your job, but that could be a way for you to start your own business. I know this firsthand. You might have lost your apartment, but that could be a way for you to pick yourself up and focus on going for that house of your dreams. You might be locked up, but that could be a place for you to meet God, a place for you to meet yourself, a place for you to be healed, delivered, and restored.

A lot of people will not understand this mindset of believing that when you are in a place such as jail or prison, you should take it as a place of blessing instead of a place of punishment.

This woman's son was alive, and since he was alive, he had a right to hope to live. The bottom line is the way you look at where you find yourself is key for your attitude in jail or prison. Your attitude in jail or prison will have a big part in your life and the life thereafter.

Joseph applied this principle when his brothers ended up being jealous of his prosperous life and the blessings overtaking his life. Due to his blessings and anointing, Joseph saw his brothers turn their faces away from him to the point of selling him out to the enemies. But everywhere Joseph found himself, either in the pit or in the prison, Joseph never allowed bitterness or resentment to get to him.

With all that Joseph went through, he could have allowed himself to turn bitter, but instead, Joseph chose not to and trusted his God, and we all know the outcome. With all that Joseph went through, he had the right to become bitter, but he chose not to.

This also applies with Paul and Silas. After going around and doing God's work, Paul and Silas were put in prison to be kept and shut down. But while in prison, Paul and Silas decided not to let their circumstances and their four-wall cells limit them. Paul and Silas, being locked up and locked in, decided to not remain passive and hopeless but to sing praises unto God.

My question is this: How can we sing praises unto God while in prison? Paul and Silas were still in prison. They still faced the four walls. They were still looking at the bars of the prison's gates. They were chained up in the cell, but none of this stopped them from praising God. Paul and Silas might not have known what the outcome of their situation would be, but they sang His praises anyway.

No matter where you find yourself, never remain silent and identify yourself with your situation. Instead, as Paul and Silas show us, sing praises unto God. When they began to sing, God dispatched an angel to bring their deliverance. The very fact that Paul and Silas sang praises unto the Lord while being locked up in prison tells us that they were not concerned about their situation or limits. They did not see the four-wall cell as the end of the world; they saw their prison stay as a time to be in God's presence, which led them to sing unto the Lord.

The best way to confound the devil and his camp about your current situation is to praise God while in the situation itself.

And There Was an Earthquake

Now, I need to point out that Paul and Silas had no idea how they would be set free. They did not know how God would bring deliverance their way. They just sang praises unto the Lord, and the Lord moved, and there was an earthquake. Nobody expected an earthquake. Paul and Silas did not know that God would move in that fashion.

This alone shows that God is sovereign in His way of dealing with His people. We need to concern ourselves with praying unto Him. We need to concern ourselves with singing praises unto Him. We need to concern ourselves with trusting

God's way of doing things and trusting His promises. We must trust God, as God moves on our behalf.

Now, you might be in a prison, and you might be singing praises unto God and saying prayers unto Him. Your deliverance will surely come, but the truth is that it might not come as an earthquake, as Paul and Silas experienced. Each deliverance will come from God in its own authentic way. Your God will have His own way to deliver you. The way that God will deliver you is not as important as the deliverance itself.

Everyone Is Free

What happened in Paul and Silas's story is really amazing, because not only were Paul and Silas freed, but the foundation of the prison was shaken, and immediately, all the doors opened, and everyone's bands were loosed.

The Bible says that when Paul and Silas were singing praises unto the Lord, other prisoners heard them sing. This is very important. To have other prisoners *hear* Paul and Silas singing unto the Lord while being in the same situation as them should tell us how to behave in any situation we find ourselves in, because not only are people listening, but people are watching you handling your situation.

Now picture this with me: had Paul and Silas spent their time complaining and murmuring and being disgruntled, guess what? The prisoners would have heard or seen that as well. The prisoners heard and saw everything Paul and Silas said and did. This should be a lesson for all of us; when we go through tough times as Christians, other people observe us. During tough times, this could be a tool added to the arsenal of evangelism, because our lifestyles say and do more than what we say. Paul and Silas's lifestyle spoke louder in that prison cell than anything else.

Think about this; the prisoners heard these two men, who were in the same situation as they were, sing praises unto the Lord, and that must have shocked them to the point of receiving freedom themselves. The prisoners heard the praises that were sung, and they received their deliverance for free. They did not even contribute to their own deliverance, but they fully benefited from it.

Sometimes, what we go through is not merely for us; sometimes, it is for others as well. Everything you go through in life will never be for you alone. Understand that God's people will benefit from this too, and this is why we should be aware of people looking to us, especially as Christians. Your foundation will shake. Your doors will open. Your family and friends will be free because you are set free. The beautiful thing is that not only will they be set free physically, but mostly they will be set free spiritually.

I will repeat it again, as it is worth repeating: your attitude during tough and rough times is key to your deliverance and freedom.

Make Something out of It

Paul and Silas did not just help other prisoners get free from prison by their praises sung, but they also made better use of their prison cell. Paul wrote letters from prison. Not only did Paul write letters, he wrote letters to churches. He wrote letters to churches, and these churches were free, as opposed to in prison like him, with feet fast in the stocks.

Many Bible readers who spend a lot of time reading the New Testament read letters written by Paul the Apostle to different churches. Paul wrote two-thirds of the New Testament, and his writings are in the form of letters from a prison cell. He intended for these letters not only to encourage the churches and the Christians of that day but to encourage all of us today as well.

Paul made good use of the circumstances that he found himself in; he turned around and blessed all of us with them. Paul was placed in prison, but he did not limit himself or meddle in depression, bitterness, and low self-esteem as if the prison were the end of the world. Your prison cell is not the end of your world.

I encourage all those who are in any form of prison to not only see their prison experience as one that will not stop their life for good but also apply this philosophy that Paul did. While in prison, Paul said to himself, "Since I am in prison, I might as well make good use of my time in here and make the devil or his enemy regret his actions, and focus on blessing other people."

Live a Life That Makes the Devil Regret His Actions

One day, my pastor taught us on this topic; it was a life-changing teaching. He told us that we have to live life in a way that will make the devil and all the haters regret their actions against us. At first, I did not grab his point, but when I remembered Christ's experience on the cross, then and only then, I grabbed the revelation, and it changed my whole approach in life.

The Bible says, "Had they known it, they would not have crucified the Lord of glory" (1 Corinthians 2:8). In other words, the devil and his kingdom and all the people he used to make Christ suffer and go on the cross thought that their plan had worked, and Christ was killed, crucified, and hanged on the cross. Only then was God's plan getting ready to come to pass, and only then did the devil realize that his plan had backfired. The devil's plan backfired, and God's plan came to pass.

God's plan came to pass because Christ knew how to apply this principle. Christ knew how to make the devil regret his actions. Paul also applied this philosophy and made the devil, the woman masters, and the magistrates regret their actions. By writing letters to the churches, Paul exposed the deeds of the kingdom of darkness.

I encourage you, my readers, wherever you find yourself, to make the best of your situation while making the devil regret his actions. If you are in prison now, I encourage you to do this by enjoying the moment as much as you can and making the best use of it. Make the devil regret his actions by taking this prison experience and blessing others with what you are going through. In any prison you find yourself in, make the best of it, and make the devil regret his actions by using them against him.

If you were imprisoned for pushing drugs, then start reaching out to people involved in drugs, and bless them with advice, and counsel them on how to avoid a life of drugs. If you are or were locked up for prostitution or for soliciting prostitution, then you need to reach those who are still involved in it. With any crime that you were or are locked up for, you can start reaching out from the prison cell via that same area of crime.

One of my favorite TV shows is called *Locked Up*. I love it because it shows me the inmates' lives from a different angle. And I discovered that most of the inmates have gifts, talents, and potential, and when used or guided well, they can produce good fruits not only for them but for their families and society.

Believe it or not, prison or jail or house arrest can be a place of blessing. If Paul had not been in prison, I really doubt that Paul would have gotten inspired to write those letters he wrote. The fact that Paul was in a quiet place, in a prison cell, it was there that he had enough quiet to be inspired. Some of the inspirations one will get in life can only come from a prison cell, a jail cell, or house arrest. When one is quiet in a quiet room for more than ten to fifteen hours a day, that individual can put all his or her attention in one place, and something good can come out of it; Paul did this.

The prophet Jeremiah also applied this. In Jeremiah 33:1, the Bible tells us, "The word of the Lord came unto Jeremiah the second time, while he was yet shut up in the court of the prison." Jeremiah was in prison, and you would think that a prison is the last place you would hear from the Lord in any normal circumstance. You would think that a jail or prison cell is a place of discouragement, depression, and loss of hope. But as we all know, the ways of men are not the ways of the Lord.

There are two reasons for this point.

1. God wanted Jeremiah in prison, a quiet place, to get his full attention so He could speak to him one-on-one and Jeremiah could focus and completely hear from God and speak on His behalf to His people. God could have caused Jeremiah to hear from Him in any other way, but in His sovereign wisdom, God decided to use the prison, and by doing so, Jeremiah carried out God's heart's desire.

2. God might not have wanted Jeremiah in prison just so he could hear Him, but since Jeremiah was already in prison, shut up, shut out, and shut in, there was nothing else he could do but make better use of his current situation. This was Jeremiah's thought process: *Since I am locked up or shut in, I will not sit here and turn sad, bitter, and disgruntled, but I will live in prison and hope in God. I will open my heart and ears and see what God has to say.*

Four walls will never stop anybody from hearing from God. I will repeat my point again that nobody anywhere will stop God from speaking to you. No place and nobody can stop God from speaking to you. We see this with Paul, who wrote letters from prison, and we see it with the prophet Jeremiah, who could hear from God and spoke on His behalf from prison. Paul's prison state could not stop him from being inspired to write letters to strengthen God's people. Jeremiah's prison state could not stop him from hearing from God and speaking on His behalf. And you, my readers, I admonish you not to let your situation, whether it is a four-wall cell or any other walled room, stop you from hearing from God or even writing on His behalf to His people. There is life in prison.

Life in Prison or Jail

Usually, when you find yourself in jail or prison, the most common attitude is limited to seeing life with no hope beyond bars. One of the reasons why I wrote this book is to help awaken inmates to the fact that life does not just exist beyond bars. The truth of the matter is you can live life in jail or prison or under house arrest prior to living life beyond the bars. While in jail or prison, you might not be free to live life in public, but you might be free to live life in the cell. You might have lost your physical freedom, but you will never lose your spiritual freedom, or your mind's freedom.

While you are waiting for God to move on your behalf, and while you are waiting for your sentencing time to expire, I encourage you not to remain passive, not to remain lazy.

Take the time in jail or prison as a retreat. The jail or prison can be a place of refreshment, a place of reevaluation, a place of healing, a place of renewal. Do not see a life in prison as a wasted life. As long as you have life and breath in your body, even though in jail or prison, you can still have hope. Half your freedom might have been taken away, but you still have your other half, and since you have that half with you, you might as well use it.

As you are reading this book and maybe in a prison or jail cell, true, your freedom has been taken away, but only your physical freedom. You can still have your spiritual freedom, and this is very important for us to understand, because one's spiritual freedom will always lead that individual to exploit it. It is possible to be in a cell and still be free to think, free to expand your thought process, and free to make things happen.

Paul and Jeremiah understood this principle, and I encourage you, my readers, to apply this as well so that, even as you are locked up or locked in, you can still make good use of the freedom you have. You might be limited because of the four walls, but do not limit yourself, and especially do not limit your mind or limit your ability to make things happen from your mind.

The Blessings of Jail, Prison, or House Arrest

One would be right to ask how we can refer to a jail or prison as a place of blessings. I confirm that description is not a typo nor a mistake; we believe in this statement of truth, and we feel mandated to share it with our fellow inmates.

Let me first say this: your blessings are not contingent on your location. The blessings that God has bestowed on you are simply based on His goodness toward you. In other words, since you are blessed by God everywhere you go, those places you go become blessed. Since you are blessed, everything you touch becomes blessed.

Let me say it again: your blessings are not contingent on your location; they exist solely because God, in His ultimate wisdom, decided to bless you, and all you have to do is acknowledge that and walk therein.

Joseph applied this mindset when he found himself behind bars for no fault of his. Joseph could have held on to all that happened to him and ended up disgruntled and bitter, hating his enemies who were his brothers, or holding hatred in his heart against the king's wife who lied on him, but Joseph did not see all that. Instead, when put in prison, Joseph went in there with a good attitude; Joseph's attitude was so good and kind that the prisoners' leader put Joseph in charge of all the other inmates.

Not only was Joseph in charge of the inmates in the prison, Joseph was presented with an opportunity to use his "God-given gift" and bless the king's servants by interpreting their dreams. Joseph could have said to himself, *I am locked up, I am in a prison cell, and I have no future whatsoever, so I may as well just be like everybody else, depressed with no hope, and not give a care about anybody, including myself.*

Although he had no way out, Joseph kept his earlier dreams in the back of his mind; no matter where he found himself, he knew he was getting closer to the fulfillment of those dreams. Despite his situation, Joseph did not quit on himself nor on God. He used his gifts in the prison cell and made a name for himself.

It is worth repeating Paul's story here. Paul was in prison but decided to forget about his situation and focus on strengthening the body of Christ, or let me say a "free body of Christ." Paul wrote letters to Christians, edifying, educating, and encouraging them in their walk with Christ. Paul had an option to be selfish and care about himself, think about himself, and worry about himself, since he was locked up still, but instead, he said to himself, "Since I am already locked up, I might as well make good use of this time." Being in prison was a blessing for Paul, as he now had plenty of time to think, get inspired, and write letters to the body of Christ; this is indeed the blessing of jail or prison or even house arrest.

As we just saw, Paul and Joseph made better use of their current situation. I encourage you, my readers, to do the same. No matter how long you have been locked up, and no matter the reason behind your sentence, do not let your life end in prison. There is life in prison and after prison.

If you are alive in prison, then live life in prison. If you can still take a deep breath behind the bars, then breathe all the more. You might not have the freedom to go out and take a walk, but you have the freedom to think big and wide from the prison cell and make something happen.

The law might have taken your liberty away as a citizen, but your heavenly citizenship cannot be taken away from you. You might not be free to do what you want to do when you want to do it, but nobody can stop you from thinking any way you want. Therefore, think, get inspired, have some imagination, come up with some ideas, and get to work, because this world is awaiting you. This world needs what God has placed in you to bless others. Don't let your sentence time keep God's gift from flourishing.

I can boldly declare to you that no matter what reason got you in jail or prison or under house arrest, God can turn that in your favor and make you make better use of that time. Do not waste your jail or prison time; instead, make full use of your time in jail or prison.

I want you to search your heart and your conscious and discover what gift is in you, what God has deposited in you, and work on it. If you are locked up and reading this book, I want to advise you that if you focus on your dreams, passions, visions, and calling, only then can you make your time in jail or prison a light burden and smooth sailing. And this is the most effective way to defeat the haters, the devil, and his kingdom.

"What you meant for evil God meant for my good." All kinds of people say this commonly used and popular statement. And I pray that all my inmate readers will utter these words as well. As you sit in that prison or jail cell, you have to be able to say, "What the devil meant for evil, God meant it for our good." What your haters and your enemies meant for evil, God meant it for your good. It is one thing to be afflicted by enemies or haters or the devil himself, but it is an entirely different thing to take the affliction and throw it back at their faces and make them regret their actions. Stated earlier, and it is worth repeating, as my pastor often says, "You have to be able to make the devil regret his actions against you."

Everything you know was unfairly done unto you has to be dealt with by God Himself. As you are locked in that prison or jail cell most days, I urge you not to just get depressed and have negative thoughts. I encourage you to see this time as retreat time, as refreshing time, or as reflection time, where you have no distractions whatsoever. You have all the time in the world for you and yourself, and you can make something actually happen. Many people who are not locked up and have freedom in their daily activities will tell you that they have no time to get things done. So, in other words, when you are locked up in a cell, you have what we don't have, and that is time to focus. So make the best use of this time, and make the author of your afflictions regret his or her actions.

So far, we have dealt with inmates' attitudes in a cell and what they have to do to make their time worth it and not linger in depression and hopelessness. Now, we will switch our study to deal with inmates' life after jail or prison, and we will learn how society can relate to them.

An Inmate Life after Sentencing

This portion is the core of this book. I pray everybody reading or hearing this might be touched by God. It is true that the inmates have committed crimes of all kinds, and some have paid a heavy price, either in time served or in their life itself. We need to focus on the ones who are alive. They have served their time, they have paid their dues, and now, they are about to be free, and they are excited, or not.

With the excitement of being set free also comes sadness, because then reality hits the inmates head-on. Now, one will question how freedom from a cell can provide sadness, as opposed to joy, excitement, or happiness. The truth of the matter is that when one person spends any amount of life in a controlled environment, even if the individual made the best use of it, the person still will suffer a form of loss—lost time, lost memories, lost achievement, and so on. A lot of these losses cannot be redeemed, and when released, inmates have to decide whether to continue life from where they left it prior to checking into that cell.

Now, follow my reasoning; here, you have an individual who spent thirty years in jail for a crime he might have committed. He paid his dues. Now, he is being set free. One might think that the ex-inmate would just pick up his life where he left off and continue it. That is not possible. This ex-inmate will have to find a reasonable accommodation. This ex-inmate will have to find a way to make his ends meet, meaning he will have to find an income to survive. But while we require ex-inmates to come out of jail or prison or even house arrest and not to return there, we do not provide them with suitable means to prevent them from doing just that. Statistics tell us over and over that 80 percent of inmates return to jail or prison after being set free. It is easy for us to quote this year after year, but the solution to this epidemic is not to keep on quoting this. We have to find a solution to this issue if we really want to keep ex-inmates from returning again.

This example was of an ex-inmate who indeed committed the crime and served the time. But let us change gears and go higher. We have an inmate who served time for a crime he did not commit. He was charged with rape and served twenty-five years in jail only to be acquitted and set free. He was charged for breaking and entering into a federal building and served fifteen years in prison only to be acquitted after the real criminal owned up to this crime. My question to you is this: How does this inmate begin life again?

Let us go over what is happening now. In some instances, society can pay a restitution for those inmates wrongfully accused and jailed, but most of the time, this occurs only after charges of wrongdoing have been filed. Let me explain through an example. An individual is in prison for fifteen years for a crime he did not commit and is acquitted and set free. This individual can decide to file a claim against the federal or local government for wrongfully being arrested and jailed. Now, the federal or local government may go along with the ex-inmate and pay him off for the time wrongfully spent incarcerated.

And even at that, no amount paid for a life wasted behind bars can make up for the life itself. How much can you charge anyone for fifteen years of your life spent behind bars? Is $100,000 an adequate amount? Is $500,000 an adequate amount? Is $10 million an adequate amount? I guarantee that no amount of money can make up for your time spent behind bars, especially if you were wrongfully imprisoned.

During those fifteen years, the memories that he could have made are not redeemable. The potential that could have come to fruition is not redeemable. The education and knowledge one could have acquired during that time are not redeemable. The bottom line is no one can make up for life spent in a secluded environment. So for society to come up with any amount to try to please you for its wrongdoing is a joke, because that money can run out. And money is the answer to everything.

Now, that is the good side or good news, where the government tries to redeem itself of its wrongdoing by paying you off. But the other side of the coin is where the ex-inmate is freed after serving a long time for no personal wrongdoing and gets no form of restitution or payment. While we acknowledge that a form of restitution or financial satisfaction is possible, it is not best nor guaranteed. But we need to appreciate that because, on the other hand, you have nothing offered, where the government decides to let you go free empty-handed. Once you walk out of that prison or jail compound, your ties with the government are cut loose. You owe it nothing, and it owes you nothing. And it goes back to business as usual, while you have to start your life afresh with no governmental help whatsoever.

A New Beginning

It is a new beginning for one who has not been free for a long time. As we all know, it is extremely difficult for anyone to start anything, but it is nearly impossible for anyone to start his or her life all over again. Discouragement is now present. Depression is now present. Mental, emotional, and physical fatigue is now the norm for your life. And even after you have made up your mind to start over again, once you encounter any form of obstacle or roadblock, it will automatically tempt you to believe that it has inevitably come up because of your past, and therefore, you might as well give in and get down and out. It is not easy for our fellow ex-inmates to start their lives all over again from scratch without us providing them with the support that they will eventually find they need.

Now that we understand that the government, either local or federal, cannot be a reliable source of restoration or reinstitution for ex-inmates, it is left up to us to discover who we can rely on to help our fellow inmates. Knowing for a fact that they cannot rely on themselves to be reinstituted or restored, and wanting to help keep them from going back behind bars, we have to ultimately find a reliable source of help for them.

Here comes the Church. In many societies, anytime there is no leadership, society tends to turn to the Church. The Church was never meant to take care of the soul of a person first. The Church has always been an institution that helps a person's soul, body, and mind.

Remember when Christ had to feed five thousand men, and four thousand men the second time. That whole encounter confirms my point. Christ could have dealt with the people's spiritual needs only and ignored their physical hunger and their lack of clothing. Christ could have preached the gospel and saved the crowd and been done with them, but instead, Christ decided to feed them natural foods; by doing this, Christ shows to us the importance of being involved in people's lives on a daily basis and dealing with daily personal issues.

In general, the Church has fallen short in caring for His people's natural needs and care. The Church is quick to tell folks about their spiritual shortcomings and their need for a Savior, but while attempting to meet their spiritual needs, the Church purposely ignores their need for natural care. We can preach Christ's love all day long, but we can't demonstrate that love by only taking care of their physical needs and ignoring their natural needs. Then this gospel is not what it was meant to be.

Whether or not we like it, society must deal with inmates after they come out of prison or when their sentencing time expires. We have a choice to either welcome them back to society or turn them away, which will do us no good. In order for society to effectively welcome back inmates, we have to have the Church involved. Society is not yet a place to welcome back inmates independent from the Church. Society and the Church have to work in partnership in resolving this issue once and for all.

This is where the Church comes in handy. The Church was placed here to affect society. The Church was placed here to move society forward. As we can read in the Old Testament, kings and leaders always sought counsel from church leaders concerning affairs that they had to decide on. This is why we have to approach this jail and prison issue with the Church in mind.

Acts 12 confirms this when it says Peter was put in prison for no fault of his own but he had a support system beyond the four walls, because the Church understood this principle and applied it. The Bible says that while Peter was inside bars, the Church prayed.

The Church Prays for Inmates

The Church not only understood its role in praying for inmates but prayed without ceasing. Now, let me clarify this: anyone can pray a prayer that is good, but if that individual can pray without ceasing, that means the individual takes this personally and seriously.

When we understand the gravity of inmates' being locked up, and the importance of what is expected from us, then we need to be like the Church that prayed for inmates. We need to go beyond just praying, but we need to take praying personally and seriously and pray without ceasing. We have to pray without ceasing for our brothers and sisters who are locked up in a jail or prison cell.

The Church needs to take this personally and not rely on anybody else to do what is expected of us, the Church. Nobody else can do what the Church is expected to do. Let me say it again: the Church cannot expect society (local and federal governments) to do what the Church is called to do.

The Church applied this in dealing with Peter, detailed in the Book of Acts.

The Church prayed for Peter without ceasing while he was locked up. The Church did not concern itself with what caused Peter to be locked up. The Church did not inquire as to what Peter might have done to cause him to be in prison. We should not concern ourselves with an inmate's criminal history in order for us to get involved. Law enforcement will deal with the inmate's criminal history. There ought to be a separation between law enforcement's involvement and the Church's involvement in the inmate's life.

While the Church was praying, Peter was sleeping between two soldiers. Peter was sleeping not just for the sake of sleeping but to save energy for the escape that God was preparing for him. Not only did Peter seek rest for his escape journey, but Peter also rested in trust that God would do something on his behalf. When you know that your God will see you through, you can rest at peace. God had Peter sleep so he could save his energy not only to escape but to live life beyond bars (Acts 12:6).

As Paul and Silas had no idea how their freedom would come, Peter also had no idea how his freedom would happen. Peter did not even know that the Church was praying for him. Basically, Peter was sleeping and waiting for whatever would happen, and was eventually surprised by the way God decided to get him free: by sending an angel his way. The angel God sent to Peter directly answered the Church's prayers unto the Lord on Peter's behalf.

All we have to do as a church is pray and leave the outcome up to God. We will leave the way God answers our prayers to free inmates up to God. God, in His ultimate sovereign authority, will choose how to carry out the deliverance of His people. God can decide to have them serve time and be freed, or serve time and never be freed, or serve time for a while and then be freed. God has the last word when it comes to an inmate's freedom from jail, prison, or house arrest.

We, as the Church, ought to pray and leave the outcome of carrying out the answers up to God. We need to focus our attention on receiving our inmates back into our midst. After we pray for our inmates, after we visit our inmates, we, the Church, need to prepare ourselves to welcome the inmates back to society. If the Church welcomes back inmates, society will follow suit. Society always follows the Church.

Welcome Back

While most church leaders instruct us to pray, nobody really emphasizes the importance of receiving answers to our prayers. It is one thing to pray, but it is another thing to receive the answers to the prayers. While we are taught to pray without ceasing, we need to learn how to receive the answers to our prayers. It takes faith to pray, so it will also take faith to receive answers to our prayers.

The Church that prayed for Peter also experienced this. Even though the Church prayed for Peter's freedom, the Church was not ready to receive the answers to its prayers. How do

I know that? Because when Peter was freed and led by an angel, and Peter came to the place where the Church was gathered in prayer and knocked at the door, the maid and the church folk did not want to open the door, not believing that it was Peter's ghost, as opposed to Peter himself. They spent time praying for Peter's freedom, but when he was set free, neither the maid nor the Church could discern that it was time to switch from praying to receiving.

We have to apply this in other areas of our lives as well. Let me explain. Sometimes when we pray to God, we do not spend a lot of time preparing to receive the answers to our prayers. As we pray, we need to know how to receive as well. The Church prayed well, but the Church had to receive.

Now, I have to make this clarification here. When I talk about the Church being ready to receive our inmates back, I am not just referring to work involving the spiritual realm. There are a lot of things outside the four walls of a church building that the Church can do something about. Other agencies and private organizations out there have some programs available that the Church needs to partner with in order to help our inmates transition smoothly.

The truth of the matter is that some inmates will spend the rest of their lives in a cell, while others will be released to come back to society. While we do have some programs for the "lifetimer inmates" inside jail and prison cells, what we need to do now is focus on the inmates who will be restored into society. These inmates will have to transition back to society, and we can make that transition smoother by allowing the Church to play its original role in society.

Transition Time

There has to be room for change. We cannot expect inmates, once freed from jail or prison, to easily reintegrate back into society. We have to allow inmates to have a transition time once they are restored in society, and the Church will have to take the lead in those programs as well.

The Church has chaplains available to help with this project of transitioning inmates back to society. And society will be better off with inmates who are well trained. A well-trained, restored inmate is always better for any society. Let me explain myself. If repeat offenders or repeat inmates do most crimes, then it doesn't take magic to understand that we can change this statistic by preventing repeat actions from arising in our inmates' minds.

If we can fit ourselves in inmates' shoes, we will discover that it is not easy to go away and serve time and then be freed only to return to the same place they came from. Things could be easier if inmates could move into a different environment, where they can have a fresh start in life. It is hard, if not impossible, for an inmate to have different results if he or she returns to the same environment and deals with the same issues and the same people he or she encountered prior to going away.

If we want to see inmates flourish and prosper after serving time, we have to help them with new lodgings. The inmates must be provided with a new environment in order for them to have a new, better beginning—not only a different living environment but also an employment opportunity.

The inmates will have to be provided with something to do after they are freed—a job, a business, or a career where they can stay busy and that keeps them from going back to the areas of their old crimes. When inmates have something to do, that will potentially keep their minds occupied and therefore prevent them from acting as they have in the past.

As all of us, at one point in our lives, were granted a second, a third, and even a fourth chance, we need to extend this to inmates as well. We need to allow them to fail. We need to allow them to make mistakes. And we need to allow them to get back up and get back in the race of life. And we have to do this without holding their past against them. After they regain their freedom, they will not hit all the marks. They will do well and then mess up. They will do well and stumble.

There is definitely life after prison, and we, the Church, need to tell inmates about that life after time served. Not only that, but we also need to show them how they can bring about happiness, joy, and excitement in a newfound life. We have to provide the inmates with tools, counseling sessions, and informative meetings so that when they get free, they know how to busy themselves with things that will keep them from going back to committing crimes.

During a visit I paid to a jail, the chaplain made me aware that 85 percent of inmates are repeats, meaning they served their time and got released only to go out and commit a crime (in many instances, the same crime), get caught again, and end up serving more time. This is the cycle, over and over and over. In the meantime, society has been dealing with this for years and still cannot figure out how to slow down this issue or even resolve it once and for all.

The Church has to sound the alarm on this issue; that we cannot avoid, but we have to face it head-on.

Christ's Prisoner

Helping you go from man's prisoner to Christ's prisoner is the ultimate goal I want to accomplish with this book. Whatever is to be learned from this book, we have to understand that it all started with Christ, and it all ends with Christ. Whether we are free or we are locked up in a prison or jail cell or under house arrest, Christ is the only solution for our lives (Ephesians 3:1; Philemon 1:1). When you are Christ's prisoner, you will live your life according to Christ's principles. That will help prevent you from ending up an inmate, and it will help you even as an inmate, and as an ex-inmate once you cross those gates into a free society.

The Bible tells us in Ephesians 3:1, "For this cause I Paul, the prisoner of Jesus Christ for you Gentiles." I try to enlighten all my readers with this principle that every time we read the Bible, we have to apply not only the word of God but the principles we can deduce from it. When Paul says, "I Paul," he is really asking us to look at his life and use his life experiences as the preface of his statement to validate what he is trying to convey.

"I Paul" am the one who used to go around abusing, terrorizing, bullying, and even killing Christians, but look at me now. "I Paul" am the one who persecuted Christ's followers anywhere I found them, but look at me now. "I Paul" am the one who used to bash the word of God and worked hard to stop the spread of it, but look at me now. Now, "I Paul" am preaching the same gospel that I bashed before. Now, "I Paul" am reaching out to the same group of people whom I first discouraged from following Christ to follow the gospel. Now, "I Paul" am a prisoner of Jesus Christ. The point is no matter my background or my past, I am now a prisoner of Christ Jesus. All of us can say this and ought to say this at any time of our lives.

To escape from the prison that this life might want to lock us in, we need to be Christ's prisoner. The question that you will ask is "How do you become Christ's prisoner?" You become Christ's prisoner by first asking Christ for forgiveness for all your sins and repenting from them. Then accept Christ into your life as Lord and Savior, and then submit to Christ's lordship in your daily life by following and obeying the word of Christ, which is found in the Bible, and seek a community of like-minded believers of Christ. And whether in a cell or in a church setting, encourage others with psalms, praises, and testimonies.

One can be Christ's prisoner while still behind bars. One can be Christ's prisoner in free life too. One has to be Christ's prisoner in life so one does not become life's prisoner. Whether we are behind bars or free, let us live our lives as Christ's prisoners; only then can we see Christ's light shine in our cells, in our lives, and in our communities.

CPSIA information can be obtained
at www.ICGtesting.com
Printed in the USA
BVHW08s1128250818
525564BV00006B/211/P